The Concise Illustrated Book of
Dogs

Wendy Boorer

Brian Trodd Publishing House Limited

Published in 1991 by
Brian Trodd Publishing House Limited
27 Swinton Street, London WC1X 9NW

ISBN 1 85361 195 6

Printed in Portugal

The photographs in this book were supplied by
Animal Photography and the following photo-
graphers:
Sally Anne Thompson, front cover, 7, 8, 10, 11,
12, 13, 14, 15, 16, 17, 18, 19, 20, 21, 23, 26, 27,
28, 30, 31, 32, 33, 34, 35, 36, 37, 38, 39, 40, 41,
42, 43, 44, 45, 46; R. Willbie, back cover, 4, 9,
22, 25, 29.

All artworks supplied by Eric Rowe of Linden
Artists

CONTENTS

INTRODUCTION

The dog was man's first domesticated animal, the most useful and adaptable of all creatures. The first associations between the two species took place so long ago that a definite 'where and when' is impossible to state. We do know, however, that behind the great variety of modern dogs, from the 0.9kg (2 lb) Chihuahua to the 90kg (200 lb) St. Bernard, there is wolf ancestry. Possibly when man was still a nomadic tribesman, hunting parties and packs of wolves pursued the same prey to their mutual benefit, and the long partnership began.

There are more than 400 different breeds of dog in the world today. This book deals with 40 of those considered to be among the most popular. The wide variety of choice stems from the wide variety of uses that man has found for the dog over the thousands of years of selective breeding.

The earliest and most skilled of animal breeders were the ancient Egyptians and the early Chinese civilizations. By 3000 B.C. there were already greyhounds, mastiffs, hounds with spotted coats, short-legged dogs, dogs with tightly curled tails and tiny companion animals prized above all for their minute size.

Guard dogs, hunting dogs and herding dogs differed throughout the world. Hunting might involve stalking anything from lion to rabbit, so different breeds were required for different quarry. Herding might be of anything from reindeer to goat. Differing methods of animal husbandry and farming meant that different skills were required from the dogs involved. With the development of the sporting rifle new breeds of dog were created to locate and retrieve game. The process worked in reverse as well. With the growth of railways and the internal combustion engine, many draught and droving dogs disappeared for good, their function having been superseded by technology.

New uses are being found for the dog all the time, many of them utilizing the animal's superior sense of smell. Sniffer dogs trained to search for drugs or explosives are used increasingly in the battle against crime and terrorism. Guide dogs for the blind are another 20th century development. But the biggest change in modern times is that far more dogs are kept solely as companions or family pets rather than working animals.

Choosing a companion animal should involve more than just buying the kind of dog whose looks appeal to you. The temperament and characteristics of your pet are going to be just as important, and here a knowledge of the dog's original function can give clues towards the traits you can expect. As well as your own needs, the dog's needs should be considered. Being responsible for any animal means time and commitment on the part of the owner.

Showing dogs is a very popular pastime. The governing body which licenses shows and maintains standards is the Kennel Club. Each country has its own and there are some differences between them. The breed groupings used in this book are those of the American Kennel Club. The United States allows cropping, i.e. cutting off the ear flap. This is customary and would alter the appearance in the following breeds: Schnauzer, Boston Terrier, Dobermann, Boxer and Great Dane.

It should be noted that the heights or weights given in the individual entries refer to those of dogs; bitches in the majority of cases are slightly smaller or lighter.

CHIHUAHUA

Weight: Up to 2.5kg (6 lb)
Colour: Any colour or mixture of colours

Description: There are two varieties of Chihuahua (pronounced chee-wah-wah) – the Long Coat and the Smooth Coat. Taking average weights they are considered to be the smallest dogs in the world. Smaller dogs are preferred in the show ring but it is perhaps wise to choose a larger specimen as a pet since the very small ones need a great deal of care and attention and, of necessity, live rather restricted lives.

The breed is very affectionate and inquisitive with its owners but does not usually care all that much for strangers. One of the charms of very small dogs is the big personality which goes with the minute size, and nowhere is this more true than with the Chihuahau. Their spirited alertness and quick movement ensure that they are never overlooked.

Both varieties were developed in America from somewhat obscure Mexican originals. The head is domed with lean cheeks and a short muzzle. The large, flared ears are set at an angle to the head, and the large, round eyes should either be dark or ruby in colour (the latter is especially prized). The tail is unusual in being furry and flattish in appearance, and is carried up over the back.

The Smooth Coat variety has a close and glossy coat of soft texture. The slightly more popular Long Coat has the same soft texture of hair which, though longer, lies flat. The tail is plumed, the neck has a ruff, and there is feathering on the ears and legs.

PEKINGESE

Weight: Dogs not over 5kg (11 lb);
bitches 5.5kg (12 lb)
Colour: All colours permissible

Description: The Pekingese is a thickset, well-balanced toy dog of great dignity. This is the only breed where the male is expected to be smaller than the female and is also a breed where a leonine appearance is called for. The head of a Pekingese is massive with a broad, flat skull and a nose well pushed up between the eyes, giving a wrinkled muzzle. The chest is broad and the heavily boned forelegs are bowed.

The top coat is long, straight and coarse with a thick woolly undercoat. Unfortunately the coat required of today's show dogs is so profuse that it hampers their movement and restricts their life style. Grooming involves brushing right down to the roots of the hair. Particular attention needs to be paid to the areas where knots

quickly appear – behind the ears, under the elbows, the trousers and inside the thighs.

The popularity of the Pekingese stems from the dog's character and also from the breed's romantic origins. They are stout-hearted dogs, bold, courageous and full of their own self-esteem. They are independent in nature, not to say obstinate, but, given the chance, surprisingly sporting. The first Pekingese reached the western world in 1860 when five were looted from the Summer Palace in Peking. For centuries they had been kept and bred solely by the Emperors of China, a good enough reason for the dog's air of arrogance.

MINIATURE PINSCHER

Height: 25.5–30.5cm (10–12 in)
Colour: Red, black and tan, chocolate and tan. The very rare blue is permissible in Continental Europe

Description: The Miniature Pinscher originated in Germany where it was sometimes known as the Zwerg Reh Pinscher. Reh means roe deer and refers not only to the bright red of the coat but also to the combination of grace and sturdiness which characterizes this dog. The word Pinscher itself is best translated as terrier and this dog has all the keenness, courage and enthusiasm possessed by terriers in general.

The head is rather wedge-shaped with a flat skull and a strong muzzle. The jaws are powerful and the teeth large for a dog of this size. Such a business-like mouth is a legacy from the breed's rat-killing days and it lends a certain credibility to the natural guarding instinct possessed by the Miniature Pinscher. Not only, however, is the breed very alert, agile and excitable, it is also noisy and has a high-pitched, piercing bark.

The smart and stylish outline of the dog, combined with the breed's innate showmanship, makes it a highly successful show dog. Particularly eye-catching is the high stepping hackney action required. Despite a long history in Germany, the breed did not reach the United States until the 1930s or Britain until 20 years later.

9

POMERANIAN

Weight: 1.5–2kg (4–4½ lb)
Colours: Mainly orange (see below)

Description: The Pomeranian is the smallest of the Spitz family, all of which have fox-like heads with pointed muzzles and upright ears. Most Spitz are compact dogs with heavy, stand-off coats and plumed tails curled up over the back, and the diminutive Pomeranian is no exception. Indeed the coat is so profuse that the dogs resemble a ball of thistledown with a foxy face peering out of a ruff of fur.

They are active little dogs, vivacious and buoyant in all their movements. They like to bark, so this tendency needs restraint from the start. Coat care is not complicated but needs to be regular and thorough. Because the long, straight, outer coat tends to be harsh in texture it does not mat as easily as some other breeds with coats of comparable length. Successful grooming involves brushing the coat in layers against the lie of the hair, i.e. from the tail towards the head, and making sure that each brush stroke gets down to the skin.

The Pomeranian originated in Germany, where it was known as a Kleinspitz. These arrived in England in the 18th century and were rather large, heavy dogs – about 9kg (20 lb) – nearly always white in colour. During the following century the dogs became very much smaller and also very popular, enjoying royal patronage. A wide variety of whole colours was developed, including white, black, brown, blue, beaver and cream. The Pomeranian reached the height of its popularity at the beginning of this century when orange became the favoured colour, to the extent that many of the other colours were lost.

PUG

Weight: 6–8kg (14–18 lb)
Colour: Silver, apricot, fawn, black

Description: The Pug is one of the heavyweights of the toy group, having a short and square body with a big ribcage and a wide chest. The curled tail is one of the breed characteristics, with a double twist over the hip being the ideal. The coat is fine in texture and soft and glossy to the touch. The silver, apricot and fawn colours are more clearly defined by a contrasting black mask and ears.

The head is large and round with a short, square muzzle, the whole covered with deep wrinkles. The ears are thin and small, like black velvet in texture. The eyes are dark, large, round and lustrous, with much of the Pug's charm being expressed in their soft and solicitous expression.

It is an even-tempered dog, enjoying close companionship in a domestic situation. The coat needs a minimum of brushing but the prominent eyes and the wrinkled face do need more care. The wrinkles need to be kept clean and dry and an eye injury, however small, needs prompt and skilled attention.

The Pug's bark is loud and sonorous for its size but, because of the shape of its muzzle, it snuffles and snores a lot. The breed is a very old one, having been brought from China to Holland by the Dutch East India Company in the late 16th century. From there it reached Britain and has enjoyed several periods of great popularity.

SHIH TZU

Height: Not over 26.5cm (10½ in)
Colours: All colours permissible

Description: A number of small, snub-nosed breeds originated in the Orient, and the Shih Tzu is one of them. The name means 'lion dog'. There are several breeds with this nickname, mainly because of their connections with the Buddhist religion in which the lion has considerable symbolic significance. Since neither China nor Tibet, the homelands of the Shih Tzu, had an indigenous lion population, the little dogs bred to resemble the Buddhist lion perhaps did so more in arrogant manner and indomitable spirit than actual looks.

The Shih Tzu is a sturdy, heavily-boned dog; in Britain it is not even considered a toy dog but placed in the utility group instead. It has a round, shock-headed look with hair that would fall over the

eyes if not tied up in a topknot. It is heavily coated with a beard and whiskers which should give a distinctly chrysanthemum-like effect.

Any colour is permissible but a white blaze on the forehead and a white tip to the tail are considered highly desirable. Because of the length of the coat, daily grooming is a necessity. This should be done mainly with a bristle brush to avoid breaking the length of hair. Sponging around the eyes and muzzle after the dog has fed is also advisable.

The breed reached Britain in the 1930s and was recognized in the United States in the 1960s. It is now very popular worldwide, a tribute to its friendly nature and independent spirit.

YORKSHIRE TERRIER

Weight: Up to 3kg (7 lb)
Colour: Dark steel-blue set off by markings of rich, bright tan

Description: Although the smallest dog on record, at 283g (10 oz), was a Yorkshire Terrier, show specimens are generally about 1.8–2.3kg (4–5 lb) while pet dogs can be twice as much again. The breed is active and playful with the high spirits associated with all terriers. Despite the small size, the dog should convey an impression of being vigorous and well proportioned. The tail is always docked and the eyes are medium in size and dark in colour.

The only exaggerated feature of the Yorkie is its coat. The texture is fine and silky, and in show specimens the hair sweeps the ground. To maintain a coat of length and quality requires time and expertise. The dogs seem to enjoy the fuss and attention as their hair is gently brushed (with pure bristle only), oiled and protected by

being rolled up into small paper bundles called 'crackers'. The pet owner often finds it easier to trim the coat to about 5cm (2 in) in length all over the dog. This gives a charming effect, particularly with the traditional red bow in the topknot.

As the name suggests, the Yorkshire Terrier is English in origin and was developed in the second half of the 19th century among the weavers of the woollen mills of the north. The breed started off as fairly sizeable but the smaller dogs were greatly esteemed and fetched more money. The breed's beginnings, in the back kitchens of a weaving workforce, may very well have shaped the dog's desire to be with its owner at all times.

AIREDALE TERRIER

Height: 58.5–61cm (23–24 in)
Colour: Black and tan, occasionally grizzle and tan

Description: The Airedale Terrier is the largest of the terriers. The word 'terrier' means a dog that can go to ground after its quarry, but as far as the Airedale is concerned it is rather a misnomer since so large a dog cannot get down burrows. However, in all other characteristics the Airedale is a true terrier, being full of courage and animation, alert, confident and fearless.

The keenness of expression with which the Airedale views the world should not be confused with undesirable aggression. Although the dog should be on the tip-toe of expectation at any movement, it should also be an intelligent and controllable companion. The Airedale is both a strong and a hardy dog. The outer coat is hard, dense and wiry, and there is a shorter, soft undercoat.

To prepare the dog for the show ring, a considerable amount of work is required. Show enthusiasts do not find this tedious, but the average pet owner may prefer to brush daily with a stiff brush and have the coat clipped off three times a year.

The Airedale was a breed developed in Yorkshire during the early part of the 19th century for hunting otter. The dog still retains its fondness for water but nowadays is known worldwide as a guard dog, a hunting dog and a highly successful show dog.

FOX TERRIER

Weight: Smooth Fox Terrier 7–8kg (16–18 lb)
Height: Wire Fox Terrier not over 39cm (15 1/2 in)
Colour: Predominantly white, with some black or tan markings

Description: The Fox Terrier has been one of the most popular breeds throughout the 20th century. Like most terrier breeds, the Fox Terrier originated in Britain where it was used, as the name suggests, for bolting foxes from their earths so that they could be killed by the waiting hounds. This is one of the long-legged terriers because it was expected to keep up with a huntsman on horseback.

Its colouring was developed so that in the excitement of the kill there would be no mistaking the terrier for its quarry. The tail is carried erect and is customarily docked long (about three-quarter length) so that it forms a convenient handle for pulling the dog out of trouble. The breed therefore has been shaped by its sporting past but owes its present status more to its smart appearance and its lively, playful personality. They are restless, active dogs, quick of movement, excitable and sometimes noisy.

The two breeds of Fox Terrier are distinguished mainly by coat. The Wire Fox Terrier has always been the more popular of the two and ideally should have a coat like coconut matting. To present a dog in the show ring means hours of skilful coat shaping which can be by-passed by the pet owner having the dog clipped out four times a year. Smooth Fox Terriers, as the name suggests, have a smooth, dense coat.

SCHNAUZER

Height: Giant 65–70cm (25 1/2–27 1/2 in);
Standard 48cm (19 in); Miniature under
35.5cm (14 in)
Colour: Pepper and salt (a two-tone grey
effect), black, black and silver, black and
tan

Description: The Schnauzer is a German breed and comes in three sizes: Giant, Standard and Miniature. The last is by far the most popular of the three though it is the most recently developed. The name Schnauzer means muzzle or snout and is believed to refer to the characteristic and conspicuous whiskers possessed by all three classes.

The Standard Schnauzer is the basic breed from which the others developed, and is an old breed dating back to the 15th century. The dogs were utilitarian, guarding the farm, herding the cattle, and killing the rats in the yard.

The Miniature Schnauzer was created by mating together the smallest Standards and crossing in the Affenpinscher, thus reducing the size still further while retaining the terrier-like character. They were first exhibited in Germany in 1899. Fifty years later they were beginning a spectacular rise to popularity in the United States.

The coat should be harsh and wiry with a dense undercoat. Correct trimming makes a great deal of difference to the dog's appearance, the style and smartness of the plucked and shaped animal being in marked contrast to the unkempt original. A handy size and a pleasant temperament combine to make this dog a winner.

SCOTTISH TERRIER

Height: 25–28cm (10–11 in)
Colour: Black, wheaten or brindle

Description: The Scottish Terrier is a muscular, thickset heavyweight of a dog. Like many others of the terrier group, the Scottish Terrier's coat is sculpted before he goes into the show ring. The Scottie's smart silhouette is achieved by hours of patient skill. Daily brushing will keep a pet dog in order and the coat will need stripping off two or three times a year. Dark brindles are particularly noted for having a good coat of a dense and wiry texture.

The Scottie should give the impression of great power; though small, its weight is usually well over 9kg (20 lb). The head is long with a large nose, a flat skull and neat ears. The splendid whiskers are combed forward and the dark, almond-shaped eyes are set deeply under bushy eyebrows.

Like other terriers required to kill vermin, the Scottie has large teeth set in powerful jaws. The dog has a deep ribcage and a short back with very muscular hindquarters. The tail is thick at the root and held straight up, balancing the correct outline.

Scotties tend to be more dignified and dour than most terriers. They are reserved with strangers and have an independence of mind that can be plain stubbornness. To their owners however they are loyal diehards and this endears them to many.

17

WEST HIGHLAND WHITE TERRIER

Height: About 28cm (11 in)
Colour: White

Description: The West Highland White Terrier is one of a group of short-legged terriers which originated in Scotland. It is possible that all these breeds come from the same root stock, a common ancestor distinguished by its hardiness, strength and determination.

Since such dogs were used to go underground mainly to kill or force out foxes they had to be very muscular and flexible. These qualities are still shown in today's Westie who is an agile and active little animal with a great sense of fun. The height is important as the dog had to be small enough to squeeze into the narrow rock crevices where Scottish foxes make their earths.

Small white terriers had been known in the Poltalloch area of Scotland since about 1850, and indeed when first shown in the early 1900s they were called Poltalloch Terriers. Like most dogs originally expected to work in severe climatic conditions, the Westie's coat should be double, with a hard, straight outer coat and a soft, woolly undercoat.

The colour is set off by the dark eyes and the large, black nose. Even the pads on the feet and the nails should be black. With the correct coat texture any dirt is easily brushed out. Pet dogs need daily brushing and a professional tidy two or three times a year. Show trimming is an art needing patience and perseverance.

BASSET HOUND

Height: 33–38cm (13–15 in)
Colour: Usually tricolour (black, tan and white) or pied (a white background patched with tan or lemon or sable)

Description: France has produced more hound breeds than any other country in the world, some 34 in all. Among these there are four different types of short-legged hound. The word Basset refers to the dog's stature and it is believed that these four Basset breeds were established by retaining and breeding from dwarf specimens which occasionally turned up in normal hound litters. Bassets therefore tended to correspond in all points to the parent breed except in length of leg. The Basset that reached England over 120 years ago was the Basset Artois-Normand and this was the foundation of the present Basset Hound.

Today's dog has a great deal more substance and much heavier bone than the original. The pendulous ears, the wrinkled head, the hanging flews and the deeply set eyes combine to give the dog a soulful and lugubrious air which quite belies the happy, rollicking, extrovert nature of the breed. Bassets need plenty of exercise. They are large dogs on small legs and have appetites to match their body size.

As pets they have all the advantages and disadvantages of having been pack dogs for so long. They are not aggressive to other dogs but they do not like being left on their own and will howl dismally. They are also deaf to any command once they have found a scent that interests them.

BEAGLE

Height: In Britain 33–40.5cm (13–16 in);
in the U.S. two sizes – under 33cm (13 in)
and under 38cm (15 in)
Colour: Tricolour or pied, following those
of the Basset Hound

Description: The Beagle, a hound whose hunting ability has been chronicled for centuries, is now one of the most popular pet and companion animals. They are merry little dogs and attractive because of their adaptability. They are clean, easy-to-keep house dogs, yet very sporting and energetic in the field.

Having been a pack animal for much of its history the Beagle has the advantage of being non-aggressive with other dogs, and it is a comfortable size to fit into today's living spaces.

History tells of pocket Beagles of about 25cm (10 in) but these, alas, have disappeared.

Their equable temperament means they are good with children. However, like many other hound breeds, they are wilful, obstinate, and completely deaf when they are following a scent. Because of their historical background, hunting is a passion for Beagles and, given the opportunity, many of them will roam to satisfy the need to track and chase.

The coat is smooth, dense and short, requiring little in the way of grooming. The tip of the stern (or tail) must be white but otherwise the dog can be any recognized hound colour.

DACHSHUND

Weight: Standard Dachshund ideal weight 9–12kg (20–26 lb); Miniature Dachshund ideal weight 4.5kg (10 lb)
Colour: Black and tan, dark brown with lighter shadings, dark red, red, dappled, tiger marked, brindle

Description: The unmistakable shape of the Dachshund has made it a gift to cartoonists and the butt of a thousand jokes. Nevertheless the shape had a purpose behind it, often forgotten as today's pet snoozes by the fire. The name means 'badger hound' and short-legged hounds of Dachshund type have a long and honourable history of facing such foes underground

The breed has good scenting ability and a long head with powerful jaws for a strong grip. The short, heavily boned legs and large paws make for efficient digging. The long, flexible, muscular back aids manoeuvrability in narrow burrows as does the supple skin. The big ribcage gives plenty of room for heart and lungs and adds resonance to the dog's baying at the enemy. The latter is an important point when a dog is working underground and its exact position needs pinpointing from above. The loud ringing bark of the Dachshund is out of all proportion to its size and makes it an excellent house dog.

The breed comes from Germany where various sizes are kept to hunt different quarry from badger and foxes to rabbits. In Britain and the United States there are six recognized breeds divided by weight and coat type – Long-haired, Miniature Long-haired, Smooth-haired, Miniature Smooth, Wire-haired, Miniature Wire-haired. Possibly the most popular are the Smooth-haired and Long-haired.

WHIPPET

Height: In Britain 47cm (18 1/2 in); in the U.S. about 52cm (20 1/2 in)

Colour: Any colour or mixture of colours, the most popular being particolours (a white background with patches of other colour) but fawns and brindles are nearly as common

Description: Members of the greyhound family to which the Whippet belongs are sometimes known as windhounds or gazehounds. The former refers to their speed and the latter to the fact that they rely on eyesight to follow and catch their quarry. The gazehounds are the sprinters of the dog world and the Whippet is credited with being the fastest breed of all over short distances. These dogs are built for speed, being streamlined and symmetrical, with short, close coats, a picture of elegant power.

The head is long and lean with powerful jaws and bright, expressive eyes. The arched neck is also long and muscular. The ribcage is very deep, allowing plenty of heart and lung room. The legs are long and straight and the back well muscled and strong. The whole is finished off with a slender, tapering tail to act as a rudder.

All the greyhound family use the double suspension gallop when travelling at maximum speed. Much of the propulsion for this comes from bending and straightening the backbone, particularly in the area of the loin which should be extremely strong.

COCKER SPANIEL

Height: In Britain 39–41cm (15 1/2–16 in); in the U.S. 38cm (15 in)
Colour: Various. No white allowed except on the chest in self colours

Description: Cocker Spaniels have been among the most popular breeds with the public for the last 70 years or so. This applies to both the United States and Britain though each has a different breed under this same title. Both kinds of Cocker Spaniel score with their willingness to please, adaptability and desire for human company. Neither is much used in the field any more, being now companion animals rather than working gundogs.

The head of the American breed is very distinctive with a well developed, rounded skull and dark eyes which have a soft, appealing expression. The dog's topline has a definite slope towards the hindquarters which are very muscular. The colours of this kind of Cocker Spaniel are very precisely defined and the coat is silky in texture and very abundant. The shape of the show dog is emphasized by trimming the neck, body and tail while ears, chest, legs and underbelly are coated so heavily that the hair often reaches the ground.

The Cocker Spaniel in the United States was developed from the English Cocker which is one of the smallest of the sporting spaniels. This dog is less exaggerated in shape than its American cousin. The coat again is silky but not so abundant and there is a wide range of colours. The breed is noted for its merry nature and constantly wagging tail.

ENGLISH SPRINGER SPANIEL

Height: 51cm (20 in)
Colour: Usually liver and white or black and white, or either of these colours with tan markings, though other colours are acceptable

Description: The Springer Spaniel is a breed whose versatility has led to different types being bred for different purposes. The breed is probably the oldest of the land (as opposed to water) spaniels and the name came from their original work which was to 'spring' or flush game for falcons, greyhounds, or nets. With the development of the sporting rifle such dogs were expected to find, flush and retrieve game. In the 19th century they were known as Norfolk Spaniels because of the Norfolk landowner who kept the strain going, but they reverted to the original name of Springer Spaniel at the turn of the century.

This is very much a country dog needing a fair amount of exercise and revelling in having some work to do. The working Springer is an ideal companion for the sportsman who only wants a single gundog. It is a small, compact dog quivering with enthusiasm for its job of finding game.

The pet and show Springer is a much larger, more placid animal, being the tallest if not the heaviest of the land spaniels. It is a strong, active dog looking as though built for endurance, and should be confident and friendly both to humans and its own kind. The coat is close and straight with moderate feathering. Show trimming in the United States is radically different from that in Britain.

GOLDEN RETRIEVER

Height: 56–61cm (22–24 in)
Colour: Any shade of gold or cream. Nowadays cream seems to predominate in Britain while being discouraged elsewhere

Description: The widely known and much loved Golden Retriever is a relatively modern breed and has achieved universal popularity through its friendly nature and handsome appearance. The dog should look well balanced as well as active and sound. In particular it should be biddable with a kindly expression and a friendly and confident manner.

The head is broad with a deep and powerful muzzle capable of holding and carrying game. The nose is always black and the eyes dark with dark rims. The body shows muscular strength with good bone and straight limbs.

The tail is carried level with the back and should be straight. The coat, which is one of the dog's most attractive features, should be dense and water-resisting. It lies flat to the body with a wavy texture with abundant feathering on the backs of the legs and the tail.

All retrievers have a will to please and the Golden is no exception. The desire to fetch and carry is also built in and many have the charming habit of bringing their owners a present – carrying shoes or gloves or newspapers as a way of greeting. As well as being worked as gundogs, Golden Retrievers are used widely for guiding the blind, and are firm favourites as family companions.

IRISH SETTER

Height: No stipulated size
Colour: Chestnut

Description: The Irish Setter has raced ahead of the other setter breeds in popularity with the public. Very well-known breeds attract their own nicknames and the Irish Setter is almost equally well known as the Red Setter. This refers to the magnificent, glossy, chestnut coat, burnished and glowing in a way that is unique to the breed..

Like many other Irish breeds the background to the Irish Setter is not very clear. All the setters were developed from 'setting' spaniels which in medieval times searched for game birds such as partridge or quail. When the dog scented the game it would move cautiously, often crouching or 'setting' to indicate the bird's whereabouts.

Over the centuries other breeds were mixed in to give the original setting spaniels more speed and better scenting powers. By the 18th century the Irish Setter had been created, though most of the dogs then were red and white. The solid, rich, chestnut colour which is the hallmark of the breed today was a relatively late development in the breed's history.

Nowadays the Irish Setter is rarely used as a working gundog. As a big, racy extrovert, with an exuberant temperament and a glamorous appearance, the breed is better known in the show ring and as a pet. Many Irish Setters have the reputation of being flighty and headstrong but the demonstratively affectionate side to their character is what wins and keeps so many friends and admirers.

LABRADOR RETRIEVER

Height: 56–57cm (22–221/2 in)
Colour: Black or yellow, though other whole colours are permissible

Description: The development of the sporting rifle called for new breeds of sporting dogs, expected to find and bring back dead or wounded game. Pre-eminent among these breeds is the Labrador Retriever. This originated in Newfoundland as an active, strong, hardy, black water dog used by the cod fishermen as a general utility and hunting dog. Among other tasks it was expected to haul boats, and fetch gear and fish out of the water.

The dog reached Britain in the 1830s on the cod boats from North America, and the breed was established in Britain by the 1880s, having in the meantime died out in its homeland. Black was the original Labrador colour but the recessive yellow appeared fairly early on in the breed's history.

The Labrador should be a steady, reliable, good humoured dog of strength and stamina, although it can be boisterous and even destructive if not taught to behave. The broad and sensible head, the short, dense, weatherproof coat, and the thick powerful tail (used as a rudder and balance when swimming) are all essential features of the breed.

History has demanded versatility of the Labrador, particularly in the use of its fine scenting powers. The breed now is not only used by sportsmen but also by the police and Services for drugs and explosives searches. As a show and companion dog it is also immensely popular.

POINTER

Height: 63.5–68.5cm (25–27 in)
Colour: Liver and white, black and white, lemon and white, orange and white

Description: The Pointer is built on galloping lines. It is a dog whose outline should be a series of graceful curves and, as a large, active breed, it needs plenty of exercise. An aristocrat among the gundogs, a lot of the Pointer's class lies in the conformation of the head. The skull and muzzle are in proportion to each other and the hazel eyes have a bright and kindly expression. The nostrils are wide, soft and moist as befits a dog whose job is to range far and wide testing the air scent to find hidden game birds. The muzzle is somewhat concave, giving a slightly dish-faced look. The ears are very thin in texture and of medium length. The neck is long and gracefully arched, the ribcage is deep, the limbs straight, strong and muscular. The whole picture is finished off with a tail like a whip, carried on a level with the back and lashing from side to side as the dog moves. The coat is short, smooth and straight with a sheen of health.

The rootstock behind many of the pointing breeds is European and many continental countries have their own particular version of this dog. The Pointer is believed to have arrived in Britain from Spain in the mid-17th century. Today's descendant is an elegant thoroughbred in every way.

WEIMARANER

Height: 61–69cm (24–27 in)
Colour: Silver grey with a metallic sheen. Mouse or roe grey also permissible

Description: Germany has a reputation for producing a number of fine sporting breeds. It has always been a hunting country with a great variety of game from wild boar and deer to small mammals and birds. The Weimaraner was a breed deliberately produced in the 19th century to cope with both large and small game. The Dukes of Weimar wanted a dog that would be an all-rounder; one that would hunt, point and retrieve anything that came the huntsman's way. They also wanted something totally exclusive and distinctive.

Certainly the dog cannot be confused with any other, as the colour is unique. Oddly enough, the puppies are often born striped though this brindling disappears at about ten days old. The dog's appearance is made even more startling by the lightness of the eye colour, either amber or blue-grey.

The breed was very jealously guarded by its German owners who were reluctant to part with any. A few reached the United States in the 1930s and immediately became sought after, for they were ideal as personal hunting dogs.

The breed reached Britain in the 1950s where it is more popular as a show dog. Being bred to tackle something as big as a wild boar means that the Weimaraner is rather harder in temperament than other gundogs. This strength of mind and body has led to the breed being used as a police and security dog.

BICHON FRISE

Height: Under 30.5cm (12 in)
Colour: Pure white

Description: Small, white, fluffy dogs have always had a great appeal. The type is very ancient indeed and there is evidence all round the Mediterranean basin that such animals were prized in antiquity. Spain, Italy, Malta, the Canary Islands, all produced their own version. From the 1500s to the late 1800s such dogs were popular at most of the European courts. Then followed a decline.

Breed historians consider that there were four breeds involved in this group of little white 'shock' dogs: the Maltese, Bolognese, Havanese and Teneriffe. The last was saved from extinction by a handful of French breeders in the 1930s and re-named the Bichon Frise. The Bichon achieved a spectacular success in America in the 1970s and then became very popular in Britain, where it is placed in the Toy Group.

This friendly, happy and outgoing little dog moves with a balanced and effortless gait with the head held proudly. The eyes and nose should be black with black eye rims and black lips to emphasize the whiteness of the coat. The coat is one of the features of the breed, being fine and silky, and up to 10cm (4 in) in length. The standard suggests it should fall in soft, corkscrew curls but this is not apparent in the show ring, where the dog is shown looking like a child's fluffy toy.

BOSTON TERRIER

Weight: Not more than 11.5kg (25 lb)
Colour: Brindle with white markings

Description: The Boston Terrier is one of the few native American breeds and is often considered the national breed. They come from Boston where, in the 1860s, the coachmen of the wealthy started to breed a sporting dog with fighting abilities. To do this they used the pedigree stock owned by their employers but left in their care. The foundation cross seems to have been a Bulldog and the now extinct English White Terrier, the same mixture that produced the Bull Terrier.

Early breeding was rather secretive and it took some while for the crossbred dogs kept by the stablemen to become more uniform in type and achieve the respectability of a pedigree. The original name of American Bull Terrier was not acceptable to the American Kennel Club so they were called Boston Terriers instead.

Another early nickname of Roundhead spotlights one of the breed's distinguishing features. Although the standard calls for the skull to be square and flat on the top, the head gives the impression of being spherical, an impression heightened by the precise markings required. The ears should be small and thin and carried erect. In the United States they are cropped. The brindle and white markings of the smooth, lustrous coat have to be exact. American dogs are shown in weight categories either under or over 6.8kg (15 lb).

BULLDOG

Weight: Dogs 25kg (55 lb), bitches 23kg (50 lb)
Colour: Fawn, brindle or pied

Description: The British Bulldog was bred for the rather grim sport of bull baiting. When this became illegal in 1835, interest in the breed declined, and it was only due to a handful of enthusiasts that it was kept going. The first specialist breed club was formed in 1875 and was the first breed club of any kind in the world. The breed has been completely transformed since its bull baiting days.

On the credit side the Bulldog is now an animal of determination and tenacity whose ferocious appearance masks a loyal and affectionate nature. The head is now massive with the nose pushed back and the underjaw projecting in front of the upper. The skin is very wrinkled and the thick, broad upper lips hang down and com-pletely cover the lower jaw at the side.

The chest is very wide with the stout forelegs splayed out so that the ribcage seems to be slung between them. This makes it extremely difficult for an opponent to knock the dog off balance. From the broad shoulders and short back the dog tapers to a relatively narrow loin and hindquarters.

The movement is distinctive with short, quick steps, with the tips of the toes appearing to skim the ground. It has a short, smooth coat. The Bulldog is not a long-lived dog. Exaggerations of form have led to heart troubles, breathing difficulties and reproduction problems.

CHOW CHOW

Height: 45.5cm (18 in)
Colour: Whole coloured, usually red, though black, blue, fawn, cream and white are permissible

Description: The Chow Chow is a member of the Spitz group and there is evidence of their existence in China for well over 1,000 years. Like many of the Spitz breeds in other parts of the world, the Chow Chow was a utilitarian dog with a multitude of uses. It was used as a draught dog, a guard, a hunting dog, and ranched for its meat and fur. This past is now long behind the breed which appeared in the western world in the 18th century.

Dog shows brought the breed to the attention of the general public and the Chow's teddy bear appeal has made it very popular as a companion animal. The modern Chow is a thickset, heavily boned, rather cloddy looking dog with an immense stand-off coat. There is a smooth variety but these are very rarely seen.

Two features are peculiar to the Chow. One is the almost straight hindleg which gives the dog a stilted, jerky gait. The other is the bluish-black tongue. The roof of the mouth and the lips should also be black. The Chow has a dignified look with a broad and deep chest, powerful loins and a short back.

In an effort to make the dog appear more leonine, some of the features of the head have been exaggerated and many Chows suffer from eye troubles and have breathing difficulties in hot weather.

DALMATIAN

Height: 58.5–61cm (23–24 in)
Colour: Ground colour white with either dense black spots evenly distributed all over or profuse liver brown spots equally uniformly spread

Description: The cheerful, distinctively spotted Dalmatian is a dog that everyone recognizes. It is a muscular, well balanced and active dog of great stamina and a fair turn of speed, suitable for life with an outdoor, athletic family. On the whole the breed is neither aggressive nor noisy; the temperament should be outgoing and friendly. The coat should be short, hard and dense with a gloss on it.

The spots should not be intermingled but be round and well defined. Patches, flecking or the appearance of other colours are highly undesirable. Black-spotted dogs have black noses and eye rims and dark eyes. Liver-spotted have brown noses and eye rims, with amber eyes. Grooming is easy for the coat is hard in texture and does not pick up the dirt. Moulting is a chore since the short white hair is very visible on carpets and upholstery.

As far as we know, the background to the Dalmatian is European and the breed probably started off as a hunting dog. Seventeenth century paintings show the Dalmatian as a gundog and as an elegant pet. Later the breed became known as a carriage dog when it lived in stable yards and went out with the horses. Its good humour has also ensured it a place as an entertainer and a mascot.

KEESHOND

Height: 45.5cm (18 in)
Colour: A mixture of grey and black with a soft, thick undercoat that is either pale grey or cream

Description: When the Keeshond first appeared in Britain it was under the title of Dutch Barge Dog and the first breed club also had this title until the name Keeshond became generally accepted. The dog's role in Holland and Germany was that of watchdog and its acute hearing, alertness and loud ringing bark make it well fitted for the task.

The great waterways of Europe, the Rhine and the Dutch canals, were routes travelled by many valuable cargoes. Every barge had its watchdog prepared to raise the alarm at a stranger's footfall, and to kill a few rats on the side.

The Keeshond is a typical Spitz in shape with a wedge of a head, obliquely set, almond-shaped eyes, and small, neat, erect ears. The body is short and compact with a straight front of medium width and well muscled hindquarters. The tail is moderately long, high set and carried tightly curled over the back. A double curl is highly desirable. Movement is brisk and sharp.

The coat is harsh, straight and off-standing with a dense ruff and plenty of feathering. One distinctive characteristic of the breed is the black pencilling round the eyes, giving the dog the appearance of wearing spectacles.

POODLE

Height: Standard 38cm (15 in) and over; Miniature 28–38cm (11–15 in); Toy less than 28cm (11 in) in Britain, 25.4cm (10 in) in the U.S.
Colour: Cream, apricot, chocolate, silver, blue, black, white

Description: Today's Poodle comes in three sizes: Standard, Miniature and Toy. The latter is considered to be in the Toy group in the United States. All three sizes are intelligent, elegant dogs with a great sense of fun.

Despite popular belief to the contrary, Germany is the homeland of the original Poodles, which were used as water dogs in the sporting field. The name comes from the German *pudel* meaning

to splash. The dogs were also well known in Russia before reaching France, where their abilities as retrieving and water dogs were much appreciated.

The showmanship of Poodles was already apparent and they were widely used as entertainers and circus performers. It became a tradition to clip the coat in fancy patterns, perhaps to help them when swimming or perhaps to increase their visual appeal. The Poodle at this stage was about 50cm (20 in) in height. Mating the smaller specimens together reduced the size to under 38cm (15 in) and the Miniature Poodle came into being.

The Standard Poodle became much larger, with no upper size limit. The Toy Poodle was the last to be created as it proved quite difficult to reduce the size to below 25cm (10 in)–27cm (11 in) without sacrificing soundness and health. Delightful as the breed is, it should not be forgotten that the dense, profuse, curly coat needs a great deal of expertise.

Height: 56–61cm (22–24 in)
Colour: Fawn, brindle or red. White markings are acceptable but should not exceed one third of the ground colour

Description: Boxers are boisterous, athletic, energetic dogs that like to play the clown and sometimes don't know their own strength. They are guard dogs, territorially minded and protective of their own; some European countries use them as police dogs and border guards. The working Boxer is somewhat plainer and more serious minded than its show ring counterpart. Darker colours without flashy white markings better suit those whose job of law enforcement sometimes demands concealment and surprise.

The Boxer is a modern breed, first appearing at the end of the last century. It is a dog that belongs to the mastiff group, having the typical broad head with the short muzzle and undershot jaw. The German breeders who created the Boxer are believed to have used for their foundation the Bullenbeisser, one of the continental bull-baiting dogs.

Today's breed is a big dog, statuesque and eye-catching when in show pose. The body is square in profile and the muscles should all stand out noticeably under the skin. The dog's movement should show a powerful, ground-covering stride. The coat is short and glossy. The tail is docked short, and the ears are cropped in countries which still allow this.

DOBERMANN

Height: 68.5cm (27 in)
Colour: Usually black and tan, though brown, blue or fawn, all with tan markings, are also permissible

Description: It is rare for one man to create a breed, and rarer still for that breed to become popular worldwide. Towards the end of the last century Herr Louis Dobermann, a German tax collector, decided he wanted a guard dog unsurpassed for its quick reactions and suspicious temperament. He set to work to create a breed to his own specifications and so successful was he that by the 1920s the Dobermann had spread across the continent of Europe and was beginning to make its mark in the United States.

Surprisingly, Dobermanns did not reach Britain until the 1950s, but they quickly joined the top ranks when they did. The original Dobermann was a smaller, coarser dog than today's version, which is elegant, muscular and agile. The temperament too was a great deal sharper and less controllable. It was recognized by breeders fairly early on that so fiery and aggressive a character was a distinct liability and they bred for something calmer.

Today's dog is extremely alert, watchful and protective. They are a breed distinguished by quickness of mind and body. Their reactions are extremely fast and, although they are intelligent and trainable, this can lead to difficulties of control.

GREAT DANE

Height: Minimum – dogs 76cm (30 in), bitches 71cm (28 in)
Colour: Brindle, fawn, blue, black or harlequin

Description: Among the giant breeds the Great Dane is one of the most impressive and widely kept. With its height and a minimum weight of 54kg (120 lb), the Great Dane is both majestic and elegantly built. It is described as being a kindly dog without nervousness, one that has dignity yet a look of dash and daring, of being ready to go anywhere and do anything.

The harlequin looks spectacular but is also very difficult to breed. The background colour of the short, sleek coat is pure white and the dog is covered with black or blue patches, the edges of which give the appearance of being torn.

The correct rearing of giant breeds like Great Danes is somewhat of an art. Not only must the food be abundant and of the highest quality but regular exercise needs to be controlled until the bones and joints are well formed. An overweight puppy places too much strain on bones and tendons whereas one not fed enough cannot realize its full size potential.

Training should also begin early since man-handling an adult Dane is not a practical proposition. Danes were first shown in Germany 130 years ago, and have gone from strength to strength ever since.

ROTTWEILER

Height: 63.5–68.5cm (25–27 in)
Colour: Black with tan markings

Description: The Rottweiler is one of the mastiff breeds, all of which are distinguished by their power and weight, and their broad heads with deep and strong muzzles. Mastiffs are a very early type of dog well known to the ancient Greeks and the Assyrians. They were valued for their courage in defending their master's property, and renowned for the ferocity with which they could attack.

The Rottweiler takes its name from the town of Rottweil in Germany where it used to be a butcher's dog, driving cattle to and from market, pulling carts of produce and guarding its master's money tied in a purse round its neck.

With the advent of railways, cattle droving became a thing of the past and the Rottweiler declined in numbers until, at the beginning of this century, the Germans realized that it would make an ideal police dog. The breed did not make an impact anywhere else until after the Second World War when it became popular both in Britain and the United States.

The Rottweiler is described as a stalwart dog combining great strength with manoeuvrability and endurance. The dog should have the calm gaze of confident self assurance. Like all the breeds with a strong, natural, guarding instinct, Rottweilers need training so that they are always under control whatever the circumstances.

SAMOYED

Description: The Samoyed is one of the most spectacular and popular of the Spitz group. Originally the breed was the working dog of a nomadic people called the Samoyed who wandered in the Arctic tundra between the Ural Mountains and the river Ob. The dogs were used to herd and protect the reindeer kept by these tribes, and also to haul the nomads' possessions when they broke camp.

Early travellers who made contact with the Samoyed people spoke of their evident fondness for their dogs, who were allowed to share their hide tents and eat and sleep as members of the family. Perhaps this early integration is why the Samoyed seems less aloof

Height: In Britain 51–56cm (20–22 in), rather more in the U.S.
Colour: White, white and biscuit, or cream. The harsh, outer coat should be silver tipped

than other large members of the Spitz group. They are affectionate dogs as well as being strong, active and graceful.

The head is wedge-shaped with black nose, eye rims and lips. As if emphasizing the breed's friendliness the lips should have a slight upward curve at the corner of the mouth, giving the dog a smiling expression. The body is medium in length, not so compact as to limit freedom of movement, and not so long as to indicate weakness. Early Samoyeds came in many colours but white, white and biscuit, or cream are the only permissible colours now.

SIBERIAN HUSKY

Height: 53–59.5cm (21–23½ in)
Colour: All colours and markings are allowed but shades of wolf, silver grey and black, all with white points, are most usual

Description: Until relatively recently the Husky provided the only means of transport in the Arctic. Different tribes of native peoples developed their own types, dogs peculiarly suited to the local conditions. One such people were the nomadic Chukchi who roamed the frozen areas of northeast Asia. Their dogs were medium sized, quick and light on their feet, combining power and speed.

At the beginning of this century dogs bought from the Chukchi and thereafter called Siberian Huskies were raced in the All Alaska Sweepstakes. They were greeted with derision by other dog team drivers who considered the Siberians too lightweight to pose a challenge. However their wins forced recognition of the breed's unique qualities as a fast draught dog.

Since then the Siberian Husky has become well known as a companion animal and show dog, while the sport of dog team racing has also spread with wheeled sleds being used where snow is non-existent.

Being a dog of the north, the Siberian Husky has a particularly dense double coat which should not obscure its clean-cut outline. Cap and mask-line markings on the head are common. One startling characteristic is the bright blue eyes possessed by some of these dogs.

Description: There are many varieties of sheepdogs spread right across Europe. Each country has its own type and the Scottish representative is the Bearded Collie. Sheep and cattle dogs work in different ways in different parts of the world as animal husbandry, the terrain, and farming customs all vary.

Ancestors of the Bearded Collie were first used for cattle droving. Farmers in the mountainous areas of Scotland raised beef cattle which were driven south every year to be fattened and slaughtered. When sheep reached the highlands of Scotland, the

BEARDED COLLIE

Height: 53–56cm (21–22 in)
Colour: Slate grey, reddish fawn, black, blue, all shades of grey, brown and sandy, with or without white collie markings

dogs were used for hill gathering instead. This means that underneath the shaggy coat the Beardie is built to travel fast over very rough terrain, preferably barking as it does so.

The dog is a lean and active one, strongly made, lively and self confident. It enjoys life to the full, never becomes middle aged, and only slows down slightly in old age. Its fun-loving attitude and exuberance can either be enjoyable or tiresome, according to one's mood. The double coat should be weatherproof with the harsh outer coat keeping the dog dry. Beardies are very responsive and easy to teach. They will also use their own initiative.

GERMAN SHEPHERD (ALSATIAN)

Height: 61–66 cm (24–26 in)
Colour: Black, black and gold or shades of grey are preferred. Light colours are undesirable

Description: The German Shepherd is one of the great modern breeds. The dog was developed in Germany about 100 years ago in an attempt to produce an ideal shepherding dog. The result was a very intelligent animal capable of working independently. Both guarding and herding seem to come naturally but the dog is also very responsive to training. As a result the German Shepherd is much in demand as a police dog, army dog, search and rescue dog, or guide dog for the blind. In fact for nearly everything that a trained dog is needed, a German Shepherd will be found to fit the bill.

The ideal temperament is a steady, calm and positive one. The dog should appear self-assured, displaying loyalty and affection to those it knows, and remaining aloof from strangers. A continual watchfulness is the hallmark of the German Shepherd. The dogs were originally required to keep the flocks left in their charge on the unfenced pasture and out of the crops nearby. For this the German Shepherd had to show initiative and an efficient, tireless gait that it could, if necessary, keep up all day.

Obviously the Shepherd had to be an all-weather dog, so the coat consists of outer hair which is straight, hard, dense and close lying. Underneath this is a soft, thick undercoat.

ROUGH COLLIE

Height: 56–61cm (22–24 in)
Colour: Includes sable (shades of gold through to mahogany sometimes shaded with black), tricolour (black, tan and white) and blue merle (a clear, silvery blue splashed and marbled with black), all with white markings.

Description: Many dogs have left their working past far behind them and the Rough Collie is one of these. The name is a mystery, but the breed is traditionally associated with Scotland where black-faced sheep were common and 'col' is the Anglo-Saxon for black, so the explanation may lie there. By the mid-19th century when dog shows started, the breed was already beginning to show the glamour that took it straight to the top and has kept it there more or less continuously ever since.

Immortalized in books and films, this breed has an affectionate nickname, that of the Lassie dog. Selective breeding has improved the coat, stature and colouring of the Rough Collie from its working ancestor. The breed benefited from royal patronage when Queen Victoria took an interest, and by the turn of the century very big prices were being paid for winning specimens.

The Rough Collie should appear as a dog of great beauty, standing with impassive dignity in the show ring yet having a friendly disposition to all. The dog's expression is very important. It should be sweet and full of intelligence. The dense, profuse coat is the dog's chief glory and a beautifully groomed dog in full coat is very eye-catching.

SHETLAND SHEEPDOG

Height: In Britain, 37cm (14½ in); in America about 40.5cm (16 in)
Colour: Coat colours follow that of the Rough Collie, including sable, tricolour, and blue merle

Description: The Shetland Islands are famed for producing small domestic animals, perhaps because of the meagre sustenance or perhaps because of the adverse weather conditions. The Shetland ponies are tiny. The Shetland sheep are little and nimble, and so are the sheepdogs which were bred to look after them, preventing them from straying onto the unfenced crops or falling over the island cliffs.

These small collies were brainy and quite plain and workmanlike in looks. The breed was not recognized until 1909 and then there was a lot of controversy as to whether they should be called collies or sheepdogs. This was followed by argument as to whether they should stay as they were, tiny working dogs, or become Rough Collies in miniature. The latter faction won the day and the Shetland Sheepdog became a glamorous little dog with a profuse coat of harsh, straight hair.

They are dogs with very sweet and gentle natures, self effacing and reserved with strangers. Being very responsive to training, many are seen in the obedience rings.